SCIENCE WORLD

KU-766-045

LIGHT
AND LASERS

KATHRYN WHYMAN

Franklin Watts
London • Sydney

© Archon Press 2003

Produced by
Archon Press Ltd
28 Percy Street
London W1T 2BZ

New edition first published in
Great Britain in 2003 by
Franklin Watts
96 Leonard Street
London EC2A 4XD

Original edition published as
Simply Science – Light and Lasers

ISBN 0–7496–4966–6

Design: Phil Kay

Editor: Harriet Brown

Picture Research: Brian Hunter Smart

Illustrator: Louise Nevett

Printed in UAE

CONTENTS

INTRODUCTION

Our sense of sight is one of our most important links with the world. We can see thousands of colours and shapes which help us to recognise the people, places and things around us. But our eyes are limited. Not until discovery of lenses were we able to see the things which were either too small or too far away for our eyes to focus on.

Telescopes enable us to see faraway objects such as galaxies.

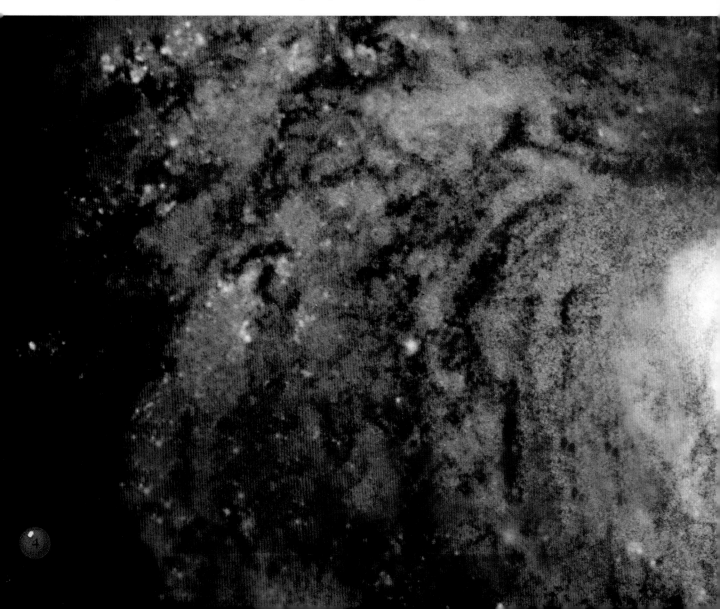

Lenses in microscopes allow us to
see tiny forms of life, helping us
to understand how living things
function. And lenses in telescopes
have enabled us to understand
something of the solar system,
and the universe, of which we are
a tiny part. In this book you will
read more about light and lenses.
And you will learn how a special
type of light, laser light, is
changing our lives.

LIGHT AND DARKNESS

Our most important source of light is the Sun. The Sun has an enormous amount of energy which is given out in the form of heat – at its centre, the temperature of the Sun is about 13 million degrees centigrade! It is some of this energy which reaches us as light.

Since the Earth spins around once every 24 hours, we only face the Sun part of the time – the time we call 'day'. At night, light from the Sun can no longer reach us. But even at night there is some light. The stars, like the Sun, produce light. The Moon also provides light. But the Moon has no light of its own – it simply reflects light which has reached it from the Sun.

Electric lights enable us to see well at night.

At night, we see how the Moon reflects the Sun's light.

How does light TRAVEL?

Light travels faster than anything else we know of. The Sun is about 150 million kilometres away from Earth and yet its light takes only about eight minutes to reach us! Some of the stars are so far away that their light takes many years to reach us. We do not see them as they are, but as they were hundreds, thousands or even millions of years ago!

Sometimes you can see rays of light from the Sun as they light up dust particles in the air. The rays do not bend – they seem to travel in straight lines.

Light travels in straight lines
Light from the torch travels through the holes in the first screen. But only the rays travelling through the centre hole have a straight path through all three screens.

Light rays travel in a straight line.

MAKING SHADOWS

Light can travel through some materials. Materials that allow light to pass through them are 'transparent'. When light shines onto an opaque object, like wood or bricks, a shadow is formed.

You can make shadows yourself by shining a torch onto the wall of a dark room. An opaque object, such as a pen, placed between the torch and the wall, will cast a shadow on the wall. On a sunny day, you can see clear shadows outside. Shadows fall wherever the light of the Sun is blocked by any opaque object.

Shadows can be used to tell the time. When the Sun shines, the pencil casts a shadow onto the base of the 'sundial'. As the Sun appears to move across the sky, the shadow falls in a different direction and points to the correct time.

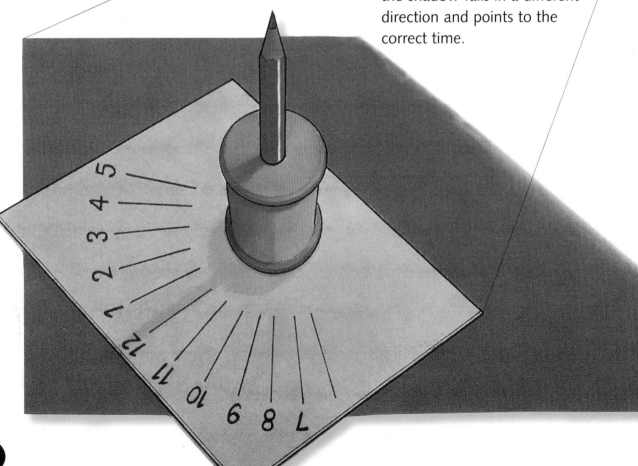

THE ECLIPSE OF THE SUN

Sometimes the Moon passes between the Sun and the Earth in such a way that all three are in a straight line. The Moon is opaque and so it casts a shadow onto the surface of the Earth. The part of the Earth in the shadow is suddenly thrown into darkness in the daytime!

If you are standing in a shadowed area looking at the Sun, you may only see part of it (a 'partial' eclipse) or it may be obscured altogether by the Moon – a 'total' eclipse.

**The light of the Sun can be blinding.
You must never look directly at the Sun.**

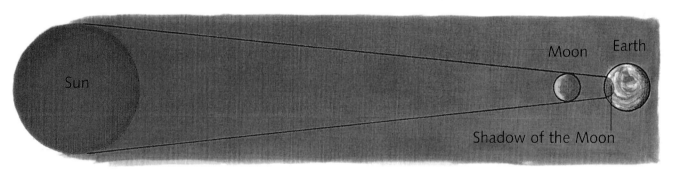

An eclipse of the Sun: the Moon passes over the Sun.

REFLECTIONS

We know that sunlight shines onto every object we see. Some of the light bounces off the object again. We say it is 'reflected'. We can only see objects when they reflect light. Most objects have no light source of their own. We see them because they reflect the Sun's light.

Every substance reflects some light. Shiny, smooth surfaces, such as metals, are the best reflectors of light. A mirror, made from a sheet of glass with a thin layer of silver or aluminium on the back, reflects light almost perfectly. However, a mirror image can be misleading. You appear the wrong way round in an ordinary mirror – left appears right and vice versa, and your reflection may be very distorted in a curved mirror.

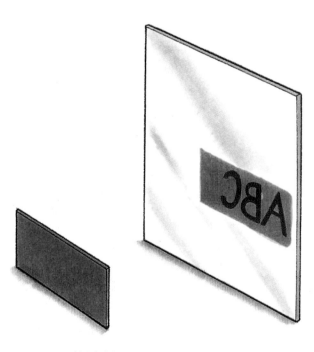

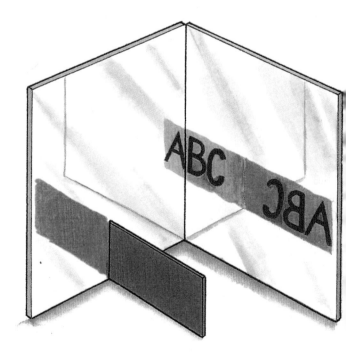

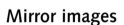

Mirror images

Letters held in front of a mirror appear the wrong way round in the reflection. We say they are 'laterally inverted'.

But if a second mirror is added, at right angles to the first, the image is turned round again.

The glass walls of this building reflect a mirror image of the street.

REFRACTION

When light travels from one transparent material to another, it changes direction. Light bends as it travels from air into glass or water. It bends again as it leaves glass or water and re-enters the air. We call this bending of light 'refraction'. The reason that light refracts is that it travels more slowly in glass or water than it does in air.

Refraction of light has some strange effects. It can make a stick look bent when it is lowered into water; it makes the bottom of a swimming pool seem closer than it really is; it can even make a traveller 'see' lakes in the desert as in a mirage.

When you look at a spoon in a glass, you see the light that the spoon reflects. Light from the spoon handle travels to your eyes in a straight line. But light from the rest of the spoon changes its speed and its direction as it passes from water to air. However, your brain assumes that the light reaching your eyes has all travelled in straight lines. You see a bent spoon which seems closer to you than it is.

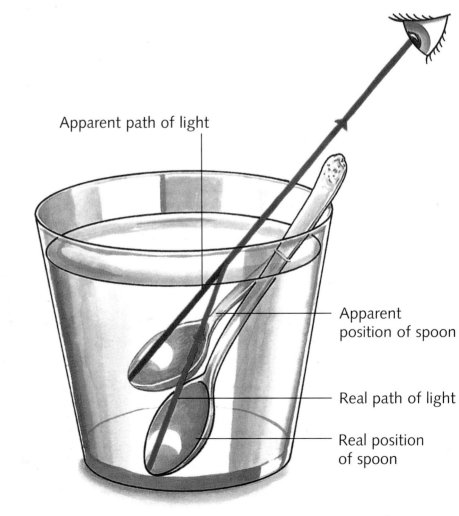

Apparent path of light

Apparent position of spoon

Real path of light

Real position of spoon

The light from this torch is travelling from cool air to the warmer air above the candle. Warm air is less dense than cold air, so light travels faster in it and bends, or is refracted. A distorted image can be seen on the screen. This same shimmering effect is produced on a hot day. Light travels faster through the hot air rising from the ground than through the cooler air above.

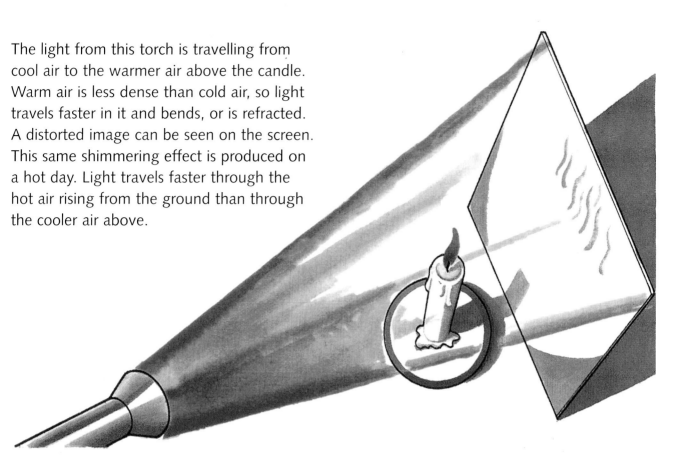

Mirages are caused by light bending as it passes through warm air.

SPLITTING LIGHT

A ray of light from the Sun, or from an electric light bulb, looks white. But this white light is really a mixture of lights of different colours! To see these colours, we must split up the white light by shining it through a glass 'prism'.

White light is refracted as it enters and leaves the prism. Different colours of light travel at slightly different speeds through the glass. As they leave the prism, they bend different amounts. The colours red, orange, yellow, green, blue and violet can be seen. They're called the 'spectrum'. We can see the colours of the spectrum naturally in soap bubbles, thin films of oil or rainbows.

You can make white light by mixing light of different colours together. This spinning wheel is divided into equal sections. Each section is painted with a different colour from the spectrum. As the wheel spins, the colours 'mix' together and the wheel looks white!

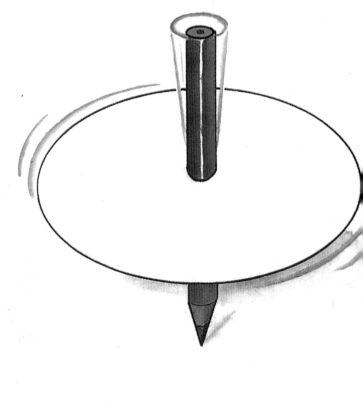

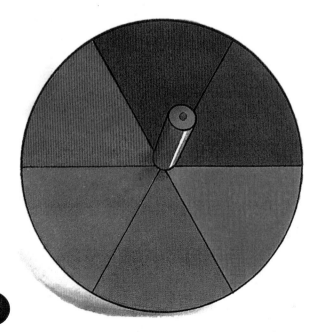

White sunlight may be split into the colours of the spectrum by raindrops. White light bends as it enters the edge of the water droplet. It is then reflected back into the drop and is bent once more as it leaves the drop. The colours of the spectrum are now spread out. Thousands of raindrops together may separate sunlight in this way and form a rainbow, one of the most beautiful natural sights of all.

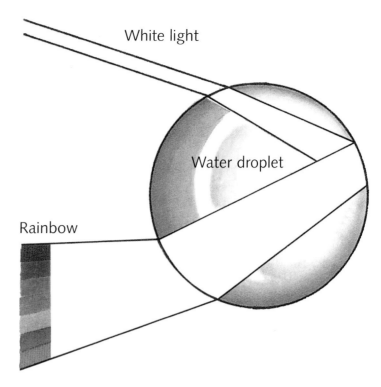

White light

Water droplet

Rainbow

The colours of the rainbow range from red on the outside to violet on the inside.

MIXING COLOURED LIGHT

Looking at this page, you are seeing the light it is reflecting. It is reflecting sunlight or electric light, both of which are 'white'. Yet you can see many different colours on the page. You must remember that white light is really a mixture of colours. The white part of the page is reflecting all the colours of the spectrum. But the printed words are reflecting almost no light. Black is the absence of colour, or light. The colours we see depend on the type of light being reflected. Red, green and blue are known as the primary light colours. It is possible to make any colour by mixing different amounts of these colours.

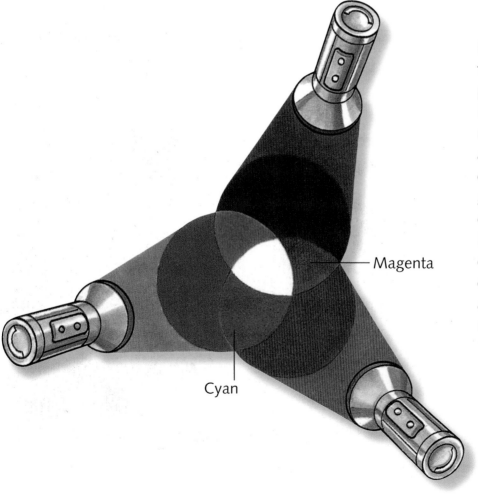

Magenta

Cyan

Here you can see some of the effects of mixing the primary colours of light. Red and green together make yellow light; green and blue combine to make cyan; and blue and red give magenta. Any other colour can be produced by varying the amounts of each of the primary colours. Red, blue and green together make white.

MIXING COLOURED PAINT

Red, blue and yellow are said to be the primary colours of paint. Blue paint reflects green light as well as blue. Yellow paint reflects green and red light. A mixture of blue and yellow paint appears green since this is the only colour reflected by both. An artist can mix paints to produce any colour.

You can mix paint to make the colour you need.

LENSES

Lenses are pieces of transparent material, such as glass or plastic, which have been made into special shapes. They refract (bend) light in certain ways depending on their shape. Lenses may be convex or concave. Convex lenses are thicker in the middle than they are at the edges. Concave lenses are thinnest in the middle.

A convex lens

Light rays from a small, close object travel in straight lines to the lens. But as they pass through the lens and towards your eye, they bend inward. Since your brain expects light to travel in straight lines, you see a magnified (larger) image.

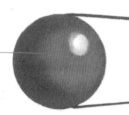

Real ball Refracted light rays

Seen from this side

Magnified image of ball

A concave lens

Rays of light from a tennis ball travel in straight lines to the lens. As they pass through the lens, they bend outward towards your eyes.

Again, the brain expects these rays to have arrived in straight lines and you see a smaller image.

Smaller image of tennis ball

Seen from this side

Real tennis ball   Refracted light rays

Convex and concave lenses are very useful. They are found in many of the instruments which help us to see things which we could not see with our eyes alone. Lenses are used in telescopes which help us see stars and planets, in binoculars which enable us to watch birds and animals in the wild, and in microscopes which magnify tiny living things.

People use lenses to carry out detailed work.

HOW WE SEE

It is light which enables our eyes to see. Light reflected from this page enters each eye and passes through a hole called the 'pupil'. In dim surroundings, your pupils get larger to let in more light. In bright light, they become smaller.

Your eyes each contain a lens. This lens is jelly-like and can change shape. The lens bends the light entering your eyes so that you always see a clear picture. At the back of the eye is the 'retina'. When light rays fall onto the retina, they cause messages to be sent to the brain. Your brain interprets the messages it receives and you are conscious of 'seeing'.

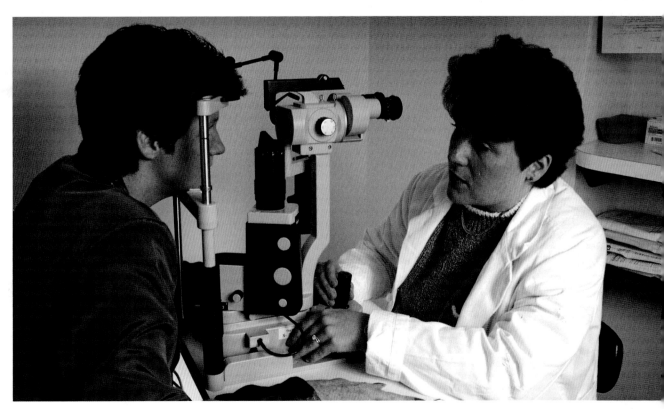

 Opticians use different lenses to check a patient's eyesight.

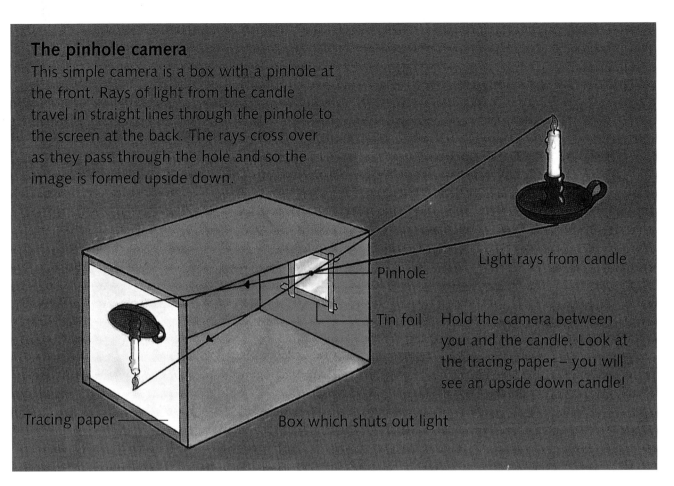

The pinhole camera

This simple camera is a box with a pinhole at the front. Rays of light from the candle travel in straight lines through the pinhole to the screen at the back. The rays cross over as they pass through the hole and so the image is formed upside down.

Light rays from candle

Pinhole

Tin foil   Hold the camera between you and the candle. Look at the tracing paper – you will see an upside down candle!

Tracing paper

Box which shuts out light

The eye works a little like the pinhole camera. An apple held in your hand reflects rays of light which pass through your eye. The lens becomes short and fat to focus the light rays onto your retina.

To focus on the apple tree, your lens gets longer and thinner. The image formed on your retina is upside down in both cases. When the information is relayed from your retina to your brain, you 'see' things the right way up.

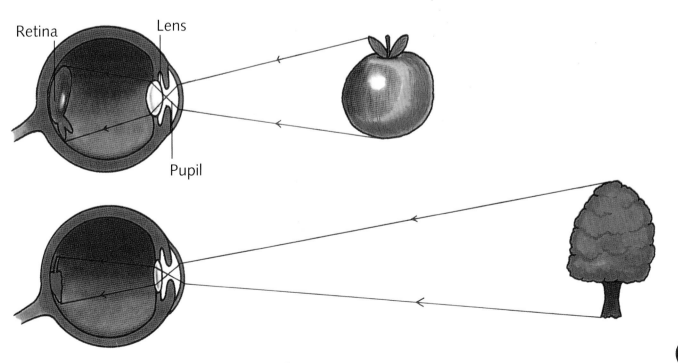

Retina

Lens

Pupil

LASERS

We have seen that white light is a mixture of many colours which can be separated. It helps to think of these colours as waves. Each different colour of light has a different length of wave. Red light has long waves. Blue light has short waves. However, the light produced by a laser is all of the same wavelength.

This means that a beam of light produced by a laser can be easily concentrated onto a tiny point. It can produce enough heat to turn a metal into a vapour! Lasers can be used to make accurate cutting tools which can even cut through diamond, the hardest substance known.

Laser light and wavelength

White light from a torch can be thought of as a mixture of waves. Each wavelength represents a certain colour. The waves making up a laser beam are quite different.

Not only are all the waves are the same length (colour), but they are lined up so that the tops (peaks) of the waves coincide.

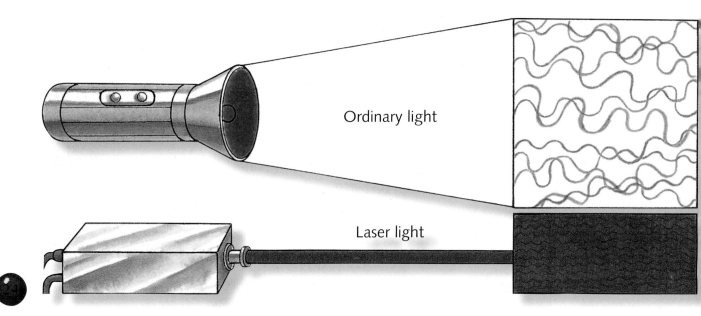

Ordinary light

Laser light

The various wavelengths making up white light can be separated by a prism. We know that laser light is all of one wavelength because it cannot be separated by a prism.

Waves of laser light are all bent to the same extent by the prism since they all travel at the same speed through glass.

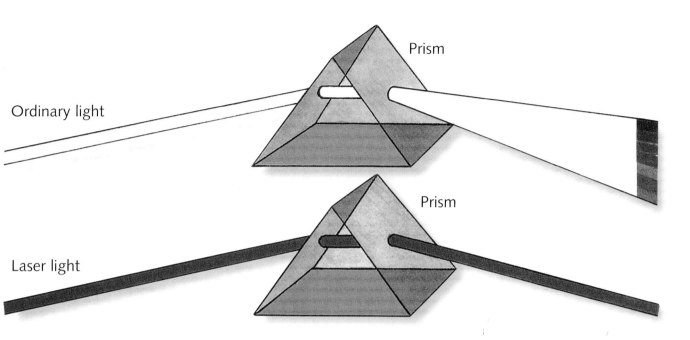

Ordinary light

Prism

Laser light

Prism

Beams of laser light are powerful enough to cut through metal.

USE OF LASERS

Lasers are one of the most important developments in recent years. There are many ways in which lasers can be used. As well as making good cutting tools in industry, lasers make excellent 'knives' for surgeons. The laser 'knife' is completely sterile and seals small blood vessels as it cuts, so that less blood is lost. Laser light is often used to 'weld' a retina, which has become detached, to the back of the eye.

Holograms are three-dimensional pictures made by illuminating objects with laser light. They look solid and real. They are used on credit cards as they are very difficult to forge.

Lasers are used in the aviation industry.

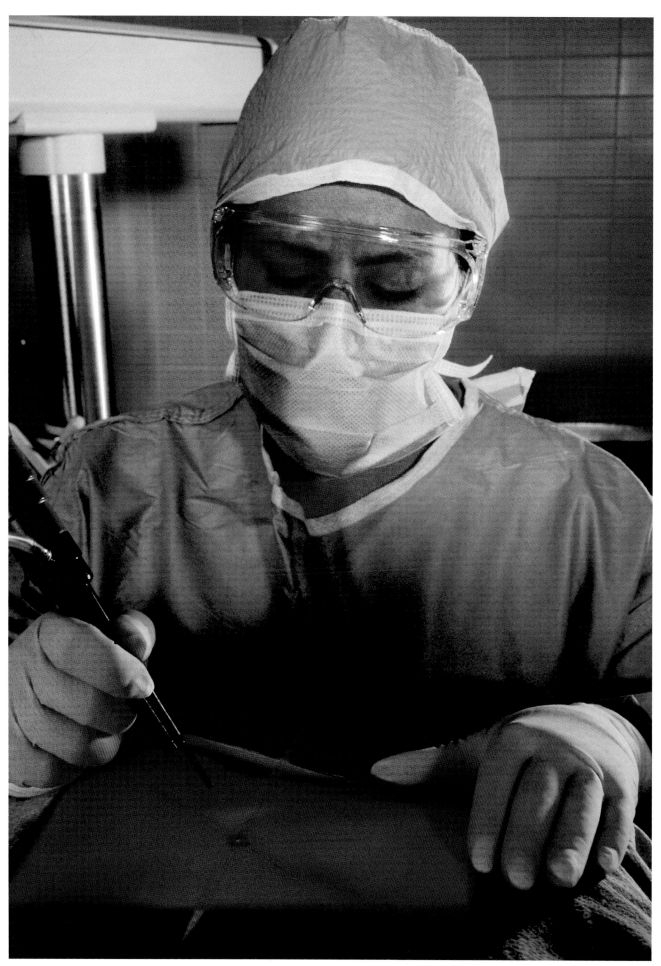

Lasers are often used in medicine, particularly in delicate surgery.

MAKE YOUR OWN PERISCOPE

This periscope is made from a box containing two mirrors held at 45°. It can reflect light so that you can see over walls and around corners!

What you need

Two small mirrors (both the same size), some card; a protractor for measuring the angles of the mirrors; a ruler; a pencil; scissors; sticky tape; and a box of paints.

Measure the distances shown as 'a' and 'b' in the diagram. Make sure that the mirror is held at an angle of 45° while you do this (a protractor will help).

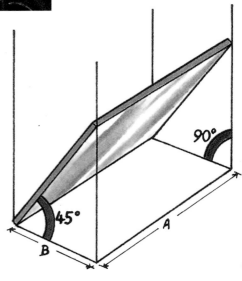

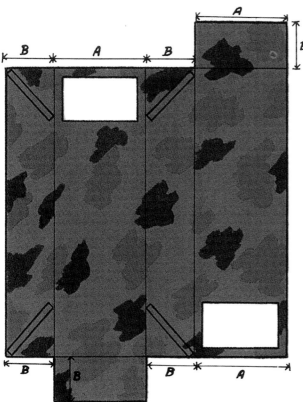

The casing

Now you can draw the pattern for your periscope onto the card. Make sure you use the measurements you have just taken. You can make the periscope as tall as you like. Cut around the outline of the pattern. Now draw two rectangles onto your box – like the ones in the diagram. Cut these out to make two openings. Fold the box into shape and hold the edges together with sticky tape.

Fixing the mirrors

Your two mirrors should fit into opposite corners of the box with their shiny sides facing the openings. Use strips of card to keep the mirrors in place, whichever way up you hold the periscope. Decorate the box as you choose. Your periscope is now ready to use. Just look into the bottom opening and see what you can see!

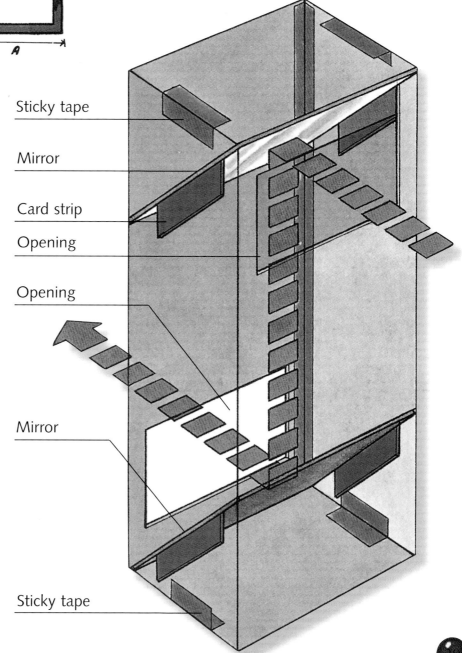

Sticky tape

Mirror

Card strip

Opening

Opening

Mirror

Sticky tape

MORE ABOUT LIGHT AND LASERS

Light waves

Light travels in waves – but what is a wave? You can make a wave by shaking one end of a ribbon. The up and down movement you make spreads along the length of the ribbon and appears as a wave. A wave is a way in which energy can move from one place to another. Light waves travel at an astonishing speed, faster than anything else we know.

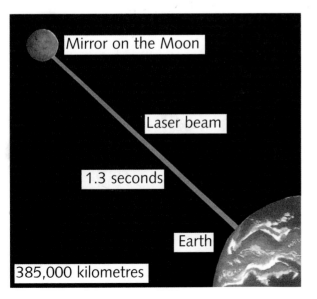

The distance between the top of one wave and the next is known as the 'wavelength'. The depth of a wave is called its 'amplitude'. Each colour of the spectrum has its own special wavelength and amplitude.

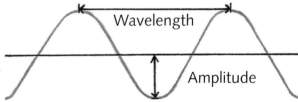

Wavelength

Amplitude

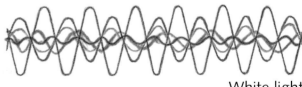

White light

Measuring with light

Both large and small distances can be measured very accurately with laser light. In 1969, the Apollo II astronauts placed a mirror on the Moon. Scientists on Earth shone a laser beam towards the mirror and timed how long it took for the beam to be reflected back again. They knew the speed at which the light travelled and so they were able to work out the distance of the Moon from the Earth – to within just a few centimetres of the actual distance!

Mirror on the Moon

Laser beam

1.3 seconds

Earth

385,000 kilometres

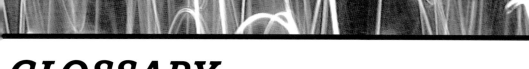

GLOSSARY

Beam
A wide band of light going in a certain direction.

Binoculars
An instrument, fitted with convex lenses, for looking at distant objects – it makes them look closer.

Camera
An instrument that records images.

Darkness
The absence of light.

Focus
Adjust to make a clear image.

Image
The picture of an object which is produced by a lens or mirror.

Light
This is a type of wave which can be seen by the eye. It is also known as 'visible light'.

Microscope
An instrument which produces a large image of a very small object. It is used by biologists to observe small living things and their cells and tissues.

Opaque
The description of a material such as a brick through which no light can pass.

Primary colours
Colours that can be combined to make all the other colours. The primary colours of light are red, green and blue. The primary colours of paints are red, yellow and blue

Prism
A block of glass with triangular top and bottom and rectangular sides. It is used to refract light.

Pupil
The round hole at the front of the eye through which light passes. The size of the pupil alters according to the light.

Ray
A narrow band of light travelling in a certain direction.

Reflection
When light is bounced back off a surface, we say it is reflected. Everything reflects some light, but flat, polished or smooth surfaces are the best reflectors. Dull, uneven surfaces can only produce distorted reflections.

Refraction
When light passes from one material to another, its direction changes. We say that the light is being refracted. Refraction takes place because light travels faster through some substances than others.

Retina
The back of the eye. It is sensitive to light.

Spectrum
All the colours of visible light, from those with the shortest wavelength (violet) to those with the longest (red).

Telescope
An instrument for looking at distant objects. It is particularly useful for studying stars and planets.

Transparent
The description of a material that lets all or nearly all light pass through it.

Wavelength
Light travels in waves. A wavelength is the distance from the top of one light wave to the top of the next. We see lights of different wavelengths as different colours.

INDEX

Photocredits

Abbreviations: l-left, r-right, b-bottom, t-top, c-centre, m-middle

Front cover main – Select Pictures. front cover mt, 4tr, 7, 9, 12tr, 19 – Digital Stock. front cover mb, 2-3, 4-5, 8tr, 11b, 14tr, 16tr, 17, 20tr, 21, 22tr, 22b, 27 – Corbis. 1, 6tr, 30tr – Photodisc. 4tl, 6tl, 8tl, 10tl, 12tl, 14tl, 16tl, 18tl, 20tl, 22tl, 24tl, 26tl, 28tl, 30tl, 31tl, 32t – Phil Kay. 5tr, 18tr – Ingram Publishing. 6b – Scania. 10tr – Corel. 13 – Argentinian Embassy, London. 15 – Picturepoint. 24tr, 26tr, 26b – NASA. 25b, 27ml – Art Directors. 28tr – August Sigur/US Navy.